S0-CBL-111

ART
'06

ART p

ABOUT ISLAND PRESS

Island Press is the only nonprofit organization in the United States whose principal purpose is the publication of books on environmental issues and natural resource management. We provide solutions-oriented information to professionals, public officials, business and community leaders, and concerned citizens who are shaping responses to environmental problems.

In 2003, Island Press celebrates its nineteenth anniversary as the leading provider of timely and practical books that take a multidisciplinary approach to critical environmental concerns. Our growing list of titles reflects our commitment to bringing the best of an expanding body of literature to the environmental community throughout North America and the world.

Support for Island Press is provided by The Nathan Cummings Foundation, Geraldine R. Dodge Foundation, Doris Duke Charitable Foundation, Educational Foundation of America, The Charles Engelhard Foundation, The Ford Foundation, The George Gund Foundation, The Vira I. Heinz Endowment, The William and Flora Hewlett Foundation, Henry Luce Foundation, The John D. and Catherine T. MacArthur Foundation, The Andrew W. Mellon Foundation, The Moriah Fund, The Curtis and Edith Munson Foundation, National Fish and Wildlife Foundation, The New-Land Foundation, Oak Foundation, The Overbrook Foundation, The David and Lucile Packard Foundation, The Pew Charitable Trusts, The Rockefeller Foundation, The Winslow Foundation, and other generous donors.

The opinions expressed in this book are those of the author(s) and do not necessarily reflect the views of these foundations.

ABOUT THE LANDSCAPE ARCHITECTURE FOUNDATION

The Landscape Architecture Foundation is a national nonprofit organization whose mission is the preservation, improvement, and enhancement of the environment. LAF accomplishes its mission through information, research, and scholarship on landscape planning and design. LAF is leading a collaborative effort to improve the American environment through three interrelated programs— the *Land and Community Design Case Study Series,* the *Landscape Futures Initiative,* and the *National Center for Landscape Intervention.* These programs are designed to assist the landscape planning and design professions in meeting the public's demand for safer, healthier, and more livable communities. LAF is the only professional organization that provides a vision and a plan to meet the needs and identify the trends in landscape planning in the twenty-first century.

ABOUT THE LAND AND COMMUNITY DESIGN CASE STUDY SERIES

The Landscape Architecture Foundation's *Land and Community Design Case Studies* are a series of analytical publications by contemporary scholars and practitioners about topical issues and actual places in which design offers holistic solutions to economic, social, and environmental challenges. The goal of the series is to provide a legacy of critical thinking that will advance enlightened planning and development in the classroom, in practice and in policy.

CASE STUDY IN LAND AND COMMUNITY DESIGN

VILLAGE HOMES

A COMMUNITY BY DESIGN

3 1336 07363 1385

CASE STUDY IN LAND AND COMMUNITY DESIGN

VILLAGE HOMES

A COMMUNITY BY DESIGN

MARK FRANCIS

ISLAND PRESS
WASHINGTON • COVELO • LONDON

LANDSCAPE ARCHITECTURE FOUNDATION

Copyright © 2003 Mark Francis

All rights reserved under International
and Pan-American Copyright Conventions.
No part of this book may be reproduced
in any form or by any means without
permission in writing from the publisher:
Island Press, 1718 Connecticut Avenue, NW
Washington, DC 20009

ISLAND PRESS is a trademark of
The Center for Resource Economics.

Library of Congress Cataloging-in-Publication Data
Francis, Mark, 1950–
Village Homes : A Community by Design/ Mark
Francis.
  p. cm. — (Land and community design case
    study series ; 1)
  ISBN 1-55963-111-2 (pbk. : alk. paper)
    1. Landscape architecture—California—
      Davis—Case studies.
    2. Planned communities—California—
      Davis—Case studies.
  I. Title. II. Series.
  SB470.54.C2F73 2003
  712'.6'0979451—dc21   2003007590
                                      CIP

British Cataloguing-in-Publication Data available

Book packaging by Academy Press

Book design by Gimga Group

Printed on recycled, acid-free paper

Manufactured in the United States of America
10 9 8 7 6 5 4 3 2 1

CONTENTS

Village Homes is a neighborhood of landscaped cul-de-sacs, streets, and pathways.

FOREWORD

The magnitude of social and environmental problems has increased dramatically during the post-World War II decades. The economic engine that has driven uncontrolled development has often not been balanced by social, historical, aesthetic, or environmental concerns. Suburban development and new communities have replaced the rural landscape with retail boxes; six-lane roads are lined with parking lots and billboards; and fast-food restaurants sit next to historic buildings.

Design and planning can make a difference. In fact the body of evidence in both the natural and built environments suggests that inspired design can make a significant improvement in the lives of people and the life of our planet. From the transformation of the grittiest urban centers to the conservation of the grandest expanse of public lands, Americans have accumulated an unparalleled record of achievement in the creation of landscapes that enrich the human spirit.

The power of planning and design to connect seemingly unrelated systems and resources lies at the heart of our ability to leave a sustainable imprint on the planet. This is a lasting legacy for future generations. From urban centers to national parks, from intercity greenways to neighborhood playgrounds, landscape planning and design is one of the most effective, economical, and valuable methods of holistically addressing such topical issues as clean water, transportation patterns, open space protection, and community planning.

In order to solve these increasingly complex challenges, professionals and their clients need timely information on emerging issues and on innovative projects that show how and why certain approaches and schemes have been successful, as well as offer helpful criticism about their more problematic aspects. Information of this type is vital to the goals of protecting natural resources and landscapes, reclaiming disturbed lands, and creating sustainable communities that foster health and safety.

Such critical and multifaceted analysis and design, taking into account the land, history, society, economics, and land use regulations, can prevent many environmental, social, and health problems. It can also restore or improve degraded land and communities. Yet this requires planning and design of the highest quality. At the same time, high-quality design has become more difficult to achieve. Forces such as population migration and growth, and rapid urbanization, require landscape planners to assess each situation anew and bring fresh thinking, rather than old formulas, to the design of our living landscapes.

The Landscape Architecture Foundation is developing the *Land and Community Design Case Study Series* to meet this critical need. The series will enhance the skills and knowledge base of the landscape planning professions, inform public policy and land development decisions, and provide material for public education. The result will be the creation of environments with the capacity to restore and promote public welfare and health, as well as to protect and enhance the built and natural environments.

L. Susan Everett
Executive Director
Landscape Architecture Foundation
Washington, DC

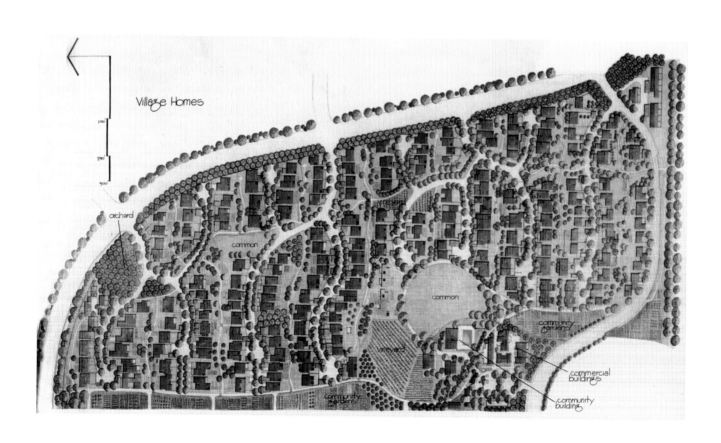

Village Homes

100
250
500

orchard

common

common

community gardens

commercial buildings

vineyard

community building

community gardens

VILLAGE HOMES:
CASE STUDY IN LAND AND COMMUNITY DESIGN

Can community be designed? For some designers, the answer may seem obvious. But for others, including sociologists, community developers, and urbanists, community does not simply result from design and planning. There are many built examples of community design, including New Urbanist designs, that fall short of creating community as the goal. While aesthetically and economically successful, they do not work as a true community society that brings people together and creates a deeper sense of place. Yet other designed communities are more successful in creating a strong sense of attachment and social interaction. The purpose of this case study is to document and critically evaluate Village Homes as one development that successfully creates community and sustainability by design. A second goal is to develop a prototype of the project-based case study for the Landscape Architecture Foundation (LAF) to advance the development of future case studies.

Village Homes is a planned community in Davis, California, and one of the most important built examples of sustainable community design in the United States. Delegations of mayors, architects, and environmentalists from around the world have visited: First Lady Rosalynn Carter came to visit in 1979, French President Francois Mitterrand arrived in a fleet of helicopters in 1984, environmental gurus such as E. F. Schumacher and entertainers such as Jane Fonda and Pete Seeger have all visited. The success of Village Homes has been widely studied and well documented. Today it is considered to be a leading model of sustainable community design.

OPPOSITE Village Homes site plan.

Village Homes, designed and developed by Michael and Judy Corbett in the 1970s, consists of 244 single- and multi-family residences on 60 acres. The community is now fully built out. Houses are planned as energy-conserving buildings around common open spaces with play areas and shared gardens. A sizable part of the development is devoted to community open space, including orchards, vineyards, and play areas. Most of the landscape is designed as an edible landscape and is owned and actively managed by its residents.

Seen early on by local planners and bankers as a high-risk development, Village Homes today is one of the most desirable and economically successful developments in California. It offers many design and planning lessons useful for community development and landscape architecture. For example, Village Homes has developed and tested innovative site design features such as open channel drainage, edible planting, and sustainable open space, and researchers have found them to be socially, ecologically and economically effective. The purpose of this case study is to make this knowledge available to practitioners and researchers as well as to provide a critical review of the project's successes and limitations as a community by design.

TOP The central open space is a large lawn for group sports such as soccer and running dogs.

BOTTOM The Village Homes playground was designed and built by neighborhood residents in 1981. The fort has been taken down due to conflicts with neighboring teens hanging out.

TOP The open space includes a major bike path connecting the residential areas.

BOTTOM Gardening is a primary activity for Village Homes residents, and is a good way to meet neighbors.

Davis, California, may be turning into one of the most innovative towns in North America in its current search for new solutions to low-energy community design.

—Rob Thayer, 1977

INTRODUCTION:

A COMMUNITY BY DESIGN

Rob Thayer predicted in his award-winning article on Village Homes in the May 1977 issue of *Landscape Architecture* that Village Homes would be one of the most innovative new neighborhoods built in the United States. Many studies since then have confirmed this. The Village Homes development has also made the community of Davis, as Rob Thayer suggests, one of the leading examples of sustainable design in the United States (2003).[1] Village Homes may in fact be one of the most innovative examples of community design since Radburn, New Jersey, was planned in 1929. Village Homes is a model community design that is unique from most current New Urbanist proposals in that it proves that open space oriented development can be effective in creating a sense of community, reducing energy use, and fostering environmental values. It is especially useful as an example of sustainable landscape architecture.

The Landscape Architecture Foundation selected Village Homes as the first place-based case study for its *Land and Community Design Case Study Series* for several reasons. Most importantly, there is considerable case study material already available on Village Homes. This includes detailed case studies prepared by the Local Government Commission, the National Association of Home Builders, the U.S. Department of Energy Center of Excellence in Sustainable Development, the Rocky Mountain Institute, and MIT's Department of Urban Planning (see websites on page 87).

OPPOSITE The focus of community life in Village Homes is common areas, each designed and built by the adjacent residents.

1 / Innovations that have made Davis recognized as an "ecological" community have often been initiated outside the university. A few days before President Francois Mitterand's 1984 visit to Village Homes, designer and developer Mike Corbett was on his bike to visit then UC Davis Chancellor Jim Meyer to explain that the French President did not have time to visit the campus and to invite the Chancellor to come out to Village Homes to greet the French dignitaries. Residents of Village Homes, including graduate students, professionals and UCD faculty members, have made notable environmental and design contributions to the neighborhood and larger community. Residents Rob Thayer, Jim Zanetto, Bruce Maeda, Virginia Thigpen, Bob Schneider, and Marshall Hunt are notable examples.

LEFT The planners laid out bicycle and pedestrian paths early on to encourage residents to bike and walk, rather than drive. The paths connect to the City of Davis greenway system.

RIGHT Passive solar design includes shading of south side of houses in the summer with deciduous vegetation.

In addition, Mike and Judy Corbett, the project designers and developers, have published extensive information on the goals and perceived outcomes of the project (Corbett 1981; Corbett and Corbett 1983, 2000). Several studies, including some useful post occupancy evaluations (POEs), have been done of Village Homes over the years by researchers, students, and governmental agencies interested in sustainable development. Much of this information is already available but is scattered in the literature on community design, energy, and sustainable development and located in archival documents, obscure websites, graduate theses, and local reports largely inaccessible to people interested in the project.

The purpose here is not to collect substantial new data on Village Homes but simply to synthesize and make available existing information in a useful and accessible case study format. A secondary goal is to show the project's significance for landscape architecture and urban design so that its features can be more easily replicated in the future. An additional goal is to provide a critical review of the project so that future work can benefit from both the project's success and its limitations.

Some brief data on Village Homes may be helpful to understand its significance as a model for sustainable community development:

• Residents report having twice as many friends and three times more social contacts than residents in a conventional control neighborhood in Davis (Lenz 1990).
• Houses use one-third less energy than other neighborhoods in Davis (Lenz 1990).
• When first proposed, the developers/designers had difficulty securing financing for the project (Corbett and Corbett 2000).
• Village Homes is now "Davis' most desirable subdivision," with homes selling at $10-25 per square foot premium in 30 percent less market time (Coldwell Banker Residential, cited in Wilson et al. 1998).

Despite its success and fame, Village Homes has not been replicated as a whole. While many of its features, such as open channel drainage and passive solar house design, have become more standard practice in community design, its holistic approach has not been more widely adopted. This raises the question of the barriers that prevent innovative community design from being more widely implemented. In the case of Village Homes, an understanding of its design and development process as well as impacts may help explain its significance and potential for landscape architecture and community design.

The designers provided a diversity of housing types, including apartments on the southern edge of Village Homes.

LAF CASE STUDY METHOD AND VILLAGE HOMES

This case study of Village Homes utilized a method prepared for the Landscape Architecture Foundation (Francis 1999, 2000). The method was developed to provide a uniform and comparable way to document and evaluate landscape architecture projects. The intent is to provide in-depth case studies about places, issues, or hypothetical situations to increase knowledge about complex problems and innovative solutions. Three types of case studies are being developed by LAF: place-based (of specific projects), issue-based (of issues that cut across projects or cases), and hypothetical case studies for teaching (to aid in training and theory development). This is the first place-based case study developed with others to follow.

The case study method involves the collection and analysis of different kinds of information, including baseline data, role of key project participants, financial aspects, project goals, and design and decision-making processes. In addition, this case study documents use, perceptions, unique constraints, project successes, and limitations. More detailed information is available in the various studies, reports, and websites cited on page 88.

OPPOSITE The eastern edge of the Village Homes development is buffered from traffic by an almond orchard, owned and maintained by the Village Homeowners Association.

Commonly owned open space includes community gardens, orchards, and vineyards.

VILLAGE HOMES CASE STUDY

This case study was developed with the following methods:

• Archival research of key documents on Village Homes

• Published reviews of past research and case studies on Village Homes

• Internet searches[2]

• Numerous visits to the community over 20 years, including behavioral observations and a short time spent living in the community

• Studies of children in Village Homes (Francis 1985, 1988)

• Tours given to visitors of Village Homes[3]

• Awards or special recognition

• Interviews with the designers/developers of the community

• Interviews with residents and users

• Interviews with nonresidents

• Interviews with maintenance people/gardeners

2 / Considerable information on Village Homes exists on the Web. The most useful websites are listed on page 88.

3 / Over the years, the author has given dozens of tours to visiting students, landscape architects, architects, planners, mayors, and environmentalists who come to Davis in search of built examples of sustainability and environmental planning. Their first reaction tends to be disappointment that Davis is a typical small university town without visible reflections of its environmental and social innovations. The suburban nature of Davis leads visitors to ask, where is the innovation? Upon arrival at Village Homes, their reaction usually shifts to amazement at seeing such a different place.

While common areas are unfenced, the fronts of houses along cul-de-sac streets are typically enclosed for privacy.

PROJECT NAME	VILLAGE HOMES[4]
LOCATION	Davis, California, located in Central Valley, Putah/Cache Creek Bioregion, 60 miles northeast of San Francisco and 15 miles west of Sacramento
DATE DESIGNED/PLANNED	1973–1975
CONSTRUCTION COMPLETED	Built in phases (50 units at a time) from groundbreaking in 1975 to build out in 1982
LAND COST	$434,000 (in 1974)
DEVELOPMENT COSTS	$2,329,241 (in 1974)
SITE IMPROVEMENT COSTS	$313,107 for swimming pool, bike paths, landscape improvements
LENDER	Sacramento Savings Bank
HOUSES	600–3,000 square foot. Also a nine-bedroom co-op house has about a dozen residents
HOUSE CONSTRUCTION COSTS	$38 per square foot (1976 dollars)
HOUSE BUILDING	60 percent built by developer and 40 percent by small contractors and owner-builders
ORIGINAL SALE PRICE PER UNIT	$31,000–$75,000
2000 SALE PRICE PER UNIT	$150,000–$450,000. Resale $10–25 per square foot higher than other sales in Davis (1995); sell in 30 to 50 percent less time than market average
RETURN ON INVESTMENT	23 percent per annum for 13 investment partners
SIZE	60 acres
PROJECT DENSITY	4 dwelling units/acre (7 dwelling units/acre not counting common landscape); 6,933 people per square mile
AVERAGE VICINITY DENSITY	3–5 dwelling units/acre; 3,458 people per square mile
OPEN SPACE	25 percent of site in public and community open space
LAND USE	244 housing units (222 single family units, 22 apartments); 800 residents; commercial office space: 4,000 square feet with 15 small businesses, including consulting and professional firms; agricultural uses, 12,000 square feet;12 acres of greenbelts and open space; 12 acres of common agricultural land; two village greens; swimming pool; community center building; restaurant, dance studio, and day care center
LOT SIZE	Approximately 4,000 square feet
LAND IN STREETS AND PARKING	15 percent in Village Homes; 22 percent vicinity
STREET WIDTHS	23 feet in Village Homes; 44 feet vicinity
AVERAGE NUMBER OF CARS	1.8 in Village Homes, 2.1 vicinity
LANDSCAPE ARCHITECT	Michael Corbett, Town Planners, Davis, California
CLIENT/DEVELOPER	Michael and Judy Corbett
MANAGEMENT	Village Homeowners Association

4 / Most of this baseline data is taken from the Local Government Commission (LGC) case study on Village Homes and checked against the Corbetts' *Designing Sustainable Communities* book (2000) and in interviews with the developers. While many sources list information on Village Homes, this data was selected because Village Homes developer Judy Corbett is Executive Director of LGC.

The Plumshire Inn includes a small restaurant, apartments, offices, and studio space for artists.

A SUSTAINABLE COMMUNITY

Visiting Village Homes for the first time, one is struck by how different it looks from the rest of Davis. While many of the houses are similar, the character of the community, is unique. Arriving by car, streets are narrower, parking less visually dominant, and access kept to the edges along long, narrow cul-de-sac streets. Arriving by bike or on foot, the neighborhood leads you along a green network of continuous paths with native and edible vegetation. It quickly becomes apparent that it is easier to walk or bike here than drive. One encounters a diverse mix of open spaces including small common areas between groups of houses, larger greenways along main bike and pedestrian paths, and agricultural landscapes scattered throughout the neighborhood with orchards, vineyards, and community gardens. Many of these spaces are not simply "look at" spaces found in more manicured and controlled development but a "lived in" landscape. There are people actually using these open spaces—walking, digging, or playing, for example. When empty, there are physical traces of use such as garden furniture, tools, and children's toys. Together this activity communicates a sense of stewardship—people caring for and feeling attached to where they live.

This is in marked contrast to the rest of Davis, with its wide tree-lined streets and more conventional development with on-street parking, garages facing the street, and fenced back yards. The City of Davis is now well known internationally as a sustainable community with its emphasis on energy conservation, bike paths, Farmers Market, natural areas, and its award-winning Davis Greenway. Yet much of this is not clear to the visitor. Sustainability is more visually evident in Village Homes than anywhere else in Davis. It is here where sustainable ideas and principles have been built and put into practice.

What is also striking about visiting Village Homes is the lack of some of the design elements now promoted as essential in New Urbanist developments. There are no front porches and front doors are often hidden at the side of houses (the developers could not decide if the front door should face the street or the common areas so they compromised and placed them on the sides of houses). The focus is on community space such as common areas, gardens, and green space rather than the public spaces of formal parks and pedestrian streets found in neo-traditional development (Brill 2002). Village Homes is as much a visual as it is a symbolic community, as Rob Thayer has observed (1989), where sustainable principles reveal themselves around every every corner.

In the two decades the author and his family have lived in Davis, the author has visited Village Homes on numerous occasions. This was the first place they lived upon coming to Davis from New York City in 1980, renting a small house on Evenstar Lane—the first street built in the neighborhood. Many friends and colleagues have lived there (Rob and Lacey Thayer, Kerry Dawson and Jim Zanetto, among them) and the author's children grew up playing with their friends in the common areas and village green. Shortly after arriving in Davis, the author was asked by a group of Village Homes' parents to help them design a playground for the neighborhood. This provided an opportunity to study how children used the built landscape of Village Homes, an inquiry he has continued over the years.

A house on a cul-de-sac is enclosed for privacy.

Architects and planners, such as these landscape architecture students, frequently visit Village Homes.

Especially informative over the years has been the large number of tours of Village Homes the author has given to visiting students, designers, and planners, many from abroad. Increasingly Davis has become a kind of environmental Mecca for foreign architects and planners who learn about it from television documentaries and books on ecological communities. It is always interesting to see their reaction when they arrive in Davis. A typical first reaction is to look a bit confused by the more standard layout of the community. While Davis has produced wonderful environmental policies and is regarded by many residents as a livable small city, much of its innovation is hidden. At Village Homes, sustainable ideas are quite visible for all to see. Walking through the lush and extensive open spaces, visitors stop to take pictures and remark on how wonderful a place Village Homes is. Many say they think this would be a great place to live. This was confirmed by one resident who commented during one of our tours, "this is not just a good place to live, it is an inspiring place to live."

Village Homes has also been a teaching laboratory for the author and his colleagues. Our landscape architecture students at UC Davis are immersed in the site planning and design principles that make the community unique, and hopefully graduate as experts in socially and ecologically responsible design. Graduate students conduct qualitative and quantitative studies of Village Homes adding to the critical evaluation of the community and its successes and limitations. Yet with all this attention and research, several questions always come up. Why does it function as a community where people know each other more than other developments in Davis? What role does resident participation and user control play in the success of the community? Most importantly, why has Village Homes not been replicated? These questions form the focus of this case study.

Village Homes innovations (such as open channel drainage) have influenced other developments, such as Aspen, California, designed by the landscape architecture firms CoDesign and MIG.

THE DEVELOPERS AND PLANNERS

The unique background of the developers helps to explain their goals in developing the project. Michael Corbett is principal in the consulting firm Town Planners, and author of *A Better Place to Live* (1981). He served as mayor of Davis in the late 1980s. Judy A. Corbett is the founder and for the past 20 years has served as Executive Director of the Local Government Commission, a nonprofit membership organization made up of almost 1,000 mayors, city council members, county supervisors and local government staff from throughout California and the Western States. Corbett served for eight years as a part-time consultant to the California State Assembly. She is co-author of a book on land use planning: *Village Homes: Solar House Designs.* She has served as a board member of the Congress for the New Urbanism since 1995. In 1999, Michael and Judy Corbett were honored as a "Hero of the Planet" by *Time* magazine.

Designers and developers Mike and Judy Corbett planned Village Homes in the mid-1970s, with the participation of residents, colleagues, and students.

Many community facilities, such as the community center, swimming pool, and playground, were built with the labor of residents.

Typical common areas.

PROJECT BACKGROUND AND HISTORY

Mike Corbett describes their early experience developing the Village Homes project. "When I first presented the concept plan for Village Homes to the then city planning director for the City of Davis, she sat back in her chair and started to laugh. 'This goes against everything I learned in planning school. Change all of it and come back and then we can talk,' she responded. What is remarkable, I was able to get about 90 percent of what was on that original plan."[5] Judy Corbett, his co-developer, has stated, "we basically had to break code in the city to get Village Homes approved" (Owens et al. 1993: 19).

And so begins the story of Village Homes in Davis, California. What started out as a visionary plan combining healthy doses of ecology and sociology eventually became an internationally recognized built example of community design. Regarded by some as a one-of-a-kind community and by others as a model for sustainable community development, Village Homes is now well known as an experiment of community planning in the ranks of Radburn, New Jersey; Reston, Virginia; Greenbelt, Maryland; Sunnyside Gardens, New York; and Milton Keynes in Britain (Howard 1965; Lang 1994; Stein 1989).

Interviewed some 20 years later, senior planner Doris Michael of the City of Davis commented, "I think the strengths of the design are the sense of community and the feeling of belonging to a neighborhood. I like the fact that there's a sense of recognition and that people care about who you are. People in this community know each other" (Fitch 1999: 15). The fact that city planners have done a complete reversal of attitude toward the project reflects both its significance in the local community and the changing culture of development today.

5 / Lecture by Mike Corbett on Village Homes at UC Davis in 1988. The fact that he was able to get the plan approved is a testament to his perseverance and persuasion.

GENESIS OF PROJECT

Village Homes began as the developers' vision in making what they call "a better place to live." Born out of social and environmental concerns of the 1960s and 1970s, Village Homes was intended as a reflection of the values of these times' environmental sensitivity and social responsibility. It began, according to developer Judy Corbett, with a small group of families meeting for a year to try to create their own community. The Corbetts later set up a booth at the first Whole Earth Festival held on the University of California, Davis, campus with sign-up sheets for anyone interested in joining them. More than 30 families met for about a year, but the group eventually fell apart. "People decided we couldn't get enough money," Mike Corbett recalled (Fitch 1999: 2).

Writing in their book on Village Homes some twenty-five years later, the Corbetts describe their early experience developing Village Homes (2000: xiii) :

> When we set out to design and build Village Homes in 1972, it seemed unlikely that we would be successful. We had no financial assets and no track record in development. We were embarking on a large-scale project that incorporated numerous untried and innovative features. The most likely outcome, and the one we expected, was that we would not succeed but would be able to publish a book about our experiences and describe how a forward-looking community could be designed. Our planning concepts and design ideas might then be useful to others. Luck was on our side. It took a great deal of tenacity and perseverance, but in the end we were able to overcome multiple obstacles and build Village Homes.

Plants grown in Village Homes are typically selected for their productive or habitat value.

The developers describe their two interrelated goals for the community: "1) designing a neighborhood which would reduce the amount of energy required to carry out the family's daily activities, and 2) establishing a sense of community" (Corbett and Corbett 1983: 1) These goals are based on a number of philosophical ideals, many combining human and natural ecology (Corbett and Corbett 2000). These assumptions help explain the philosophical underpinnings of Village Homes (see Table 1).

In the early phases of Village Homes there was a strong pioneering sense. Judy Corbett observes, "We did a lot with community work parties, building paths and foot bridges. There was a real strong 'spirit of the pioneers'; we were doing something different, for ourselves. The rest of Davis thought we were a bunch of nutty hippies. The process was very unifying socially" (Owens et al. 1993: 20). She says, "We put everything into the vision and making it work" (Judy Corbett 2000: personal communication).

This early aerial view of Village Homes shows the extensive open space, common areas, and pathways.

TABLE 1

GOALS OF SUSTAINABLE DEVELOPMENT

1. Every living thing survives by numerous and subtle relationships with all living things and with the inanimate environment.

2. Ecosystems and parts of ecosystems composed of a wide variety of species tend to adapt better to environmental changes or human tampering than do those composed of fewer species.

3. Part of the ecosystem is a complex system of energy transfers that depends, ultimately, on energy input.

4. In the long run, every one of humanity's physical needs must be satisfied either without the use of non-renewable resources or through recovery and reuse of those resources.

5. Although humans seem to be the most adaptable of living things, we still have certain inherent physical and psychological needs that must be met by the ecosystem, the human-made physical environment, and the social environment.

6. Humans are for the most part genetically adapted to the environment that existed about 200 to 20,000 years ago. This adaptation involves not just the physical makeup but also the modes of perception and behavior and relates to the social environment as well as the physical environment.

7. The relationship between people and the environment goes both ways: humanity shapes and is shaped by its environment.

8. Humans can adapt to a wide range of environmental conditions, but the results of the adaptation to inhospitable conditions is temporary or chronic stress.

Source: Corbett and Corbett 2000: 53–60.

The western edge of the Village Homes development is a bike path and continuous community garden.

DESIGN, DEVELOPMENT, AND DECISION-MAKING

Design Process

The designers/developers used a participatory approach to develop the initial planning concepts for the community. They brought together a group of friends and interested families to discuss how the project should be designed. The goals of this original group, who called themselves "the Village," were visionary:

> The discussion centered on a shared sense of dislocation, disconnection, and powerlessness and on a concern for the environment. We wondered whether it would be possible to recover some of the homier aspects of village life within the context of a modern neighborhood. We believed it should be possible to design a community so that one might live more lightly on the land (Corbett and Corbett 2000: 23).

Yet the group disbanded after a year, frustrated by the lack of a site and funds to realize their dream. The Corbetts retreated to develop their own plan and find interested investors. The final plan was their own vision, a blend of Judy Corbett's background in environmental psychology and Mike Corbett's interests in architecture and ecology. The plan was one of the first to combine natural ecology and social ecology into an integrated vision of people, nature, economy, and community.

Decision-Making Process

When the Corbetts submitted their plan to city officials in the early 1970s, it met with considerable resistance and hostility. As Judy Corbett describes the process, "Everyone had a problem. The police department did not like the dead-end cul-de-sacs. The fire department did not like the narrow streets. The public works department did not like agriculture mixing with residential. And the planning department picked it apart endlessly" (Jackson 1999: 78).

OPPOSITE The division between public and private space is often blurred, such as in this backyard.

Even the federal government found cause to question the merits of the project. "While this office is most sympathetic with your objective concerning energy conservation and environmental concerns, we feel the proposal requires further study," said Richard D. Chamberlain, area director for the U.S. Department of Housing and Urban Development (HUD) at the time, in a letter to Mike Corbett. Chamberlain questioned having apartments in the midst of single-family housing, providing parking bays instead of on-street parking, and the orientation of lots. He said the common areas seemed ill conceived, provisions for runoff of storm water inadequate, and the idea of having a homeowner association growing agricultural products questionable. "It could well be that the same objective can be obtained by enlarging individual lots and substantially eliminating much of the common area," he said, noting such a change would provide individual homeowners with space for garden plots (Fitch 1999: 2). "Our objections in connection with the foregoing matters involve the fact that, in our judgment, they deviate from accepted development practices to the extent that future marketability of residential properties may be impaired," Chamberlain concluded. "We believe that a compromise can be reached which would adequately meet your development objectives and still represent a development that would be acceptable to the public from a market standpoint" (Fitch 1999: 2).

The Corbetts responded with the persistence of missionaries rather than the pragmatism of developers. Not taking no for an answer, "they set up traffic cones in an empty parking lot to show the fire department that emergency equipment could easily navigate the narrow streets, even past parked cars. They convinced the police department that putting sidewalks behind the houses rather than in front and eliminating throughways would make residents feel safer, and Village Homes' low crime rate has proved this point" (Jackson 1999: 78).

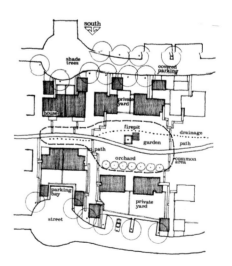

LEFT Cross section of common area with open channel drainage. RIGHT Detail of housing and common area.

The community-owned vineyard.

While city staff fought virtually every design concept, it was the political process that rescued the project and allowed it to be built.[6] Judy Corbett says, "We essentially had to appeal all their decisions to the City Council, and fortunately, the City Council was very liberal and supportive of what we were attempting" (Owens et al. 1993: 19). After almost three years of delays and negotiations, they were allowed to begin construction of the first houses in 1975.

Financing

While the plan was anything but conventional, conventional financing was needed to build the project. Judy Corbett remembered, "There was a lot of resistance to the project from local banks. We went to 30 different banks before we got a loan" (Owens et al. 1993: 21). Reasons they were turned down included their lack of past experience as developers and the unusual aspects of the plan. Eventually they convinced a bank to finance the project after downplaying its unique features.

Role of participation

While the overall plan came solely from the developers, they built in numerous opportunities for residents to participate in the design of open spaces and ongoing management of the community. One of the main ways residents have been involved is through work parties. Much of the communal landscape and buildings were constructed through this community-built process. Funds were set aside by the Village Homeowners Association to allow residents to design and build landscape areas and buildings such as the Community Center and pool. For example, each group of eight homeowners living around a common area received $600 from the Village Homeowners Association to landscape the common areas as they wished. This forced residents to work together and get to know each other almost immediately after moving in. An important benefit of resident participation is creating a sense of symbolic ownership. Surveys have shown that this participation has led to a stronger sense of attachment to the neighborhood and greater satisfaction (Lenz 1990). Other communities designed with the same principles but lacking in resident participation often do not result in such a strong sense of ownership.

---

6 / The Corbetts had been politically involved and helped get more environmentally minded candidates elected to the City Council. Without the political support of the City Council, Village Homes could never have been built.

The central open space with a small amphitheatre for gatherings and weddings.

The Community Center pool is a popular place.

DESIGN & PLANNING CONCEPTS

Village Homes combines older design and planning principles with newer, more innovative ideas. Many of its basic concepts, as the developers admit, are drawn directly from earlier greenbelt communities. The idea of a residential area organized around open space (as compared to the street) is a long-standing and popular planning concept. It also goes against most New Urbanist thinking that maintains the street as the central focus of public space (Calthorpe et al. 2000; Duany et al. 2000).

The physical planning principles grow directly from the larger mission of the community. The New Homeowners Guide published by the Village Homeowners Association (1995) summarizes the major planning concepts and spells out the social and environmental goals of the plan. "A number of design features help Village Homes residents live in an energy-efficient and aesthetically pleasing community:

- **Orientation.** All streets run east-west and all lots are oriented north-south. The orientation helps the houses with passive solar designs and makes full use of the sun's energy.

- **Street Width.** The roads are all narrow, curving cul-de-sacs; they are less than 25 feet wide and generally are not bordered by sidewalks. Their narrow widths minimize the amount of pavement exposed to the sun in the long, hot summers. The curving lines of the roads give them the look of village lanes, and the few cars that venture into the cul-de-sacs usually travel slowly.[7]

OPPOSITE TOP Village Homes is bounded on the south by Russell Boulevard and UC Davis agricultural research fields.

BOTTOM LEFT The central north-south bike path, with a wooden bridge across an open drainage swale.

BOTTOM RIGHT Bike path with orchards.

7 / The cul-de-sacs in Village Homes distinguish it from the New Urbanist communities that encourage streets on grid and do not allow cul-de-sacs. A 1997 survey done by the Urban Land Institute shows that a majority of U.S. homebuyers would prefer to live on a cul-de-sac.

• **Pedestrian/Bike Paths and Common Areas.** The common areas also contain Village Homes' innovative natural drainage system, a network of creek beds, swales, and pond areas that allow rainwater to be absorbed into the ground rather than carried away through storm drains. Besides helping to store moisture in the soil, this system provides a visually interesting backdrop for landscape design." (Village Homeowners Association 1995: 1).

Site Planning

The Corbetts list the following six elements as the main site planning innovations of Village Homes (Corbett and Corbett 1983: 27–47).

1. Community

2. Energy Conservation and
   Use of Solar Energy

3. Walking and Bicycling

4. A Design Closer to Nature

5. Neighborhood Agriculture

6. Natural Drainage

In addition, several site design and planning techniques used in Village Homes are important to its success as a sustainable community:

Village Homes is a community design closer to nature.

House design that emphasizes energy conservation.

A community plan that encourages walking and bicycling.

Neighborhood agriculture is rated highly by residents and visitors alike.

Community open space.

Open Space

A wide variety of open space types are provided in Village Homes, including private gardens, common areas, agricultural lands, turf areas for sports, and landscaped areas (see Table 2). These spaces are described in the official publications of Village Homes as "household commons," "greenbelt commons," and "agricultural lands." (Village Homeowners Association 1995: 11). Residents hold common interest in all three types of land. Common lands are specified by the Homeowners Board to be used for three purposes: enjoyment, flowers and food, and profit, from, for example, the almond orchard of 300 trees that forms a green edge along busy Arlington Street to the east. What is especially important about these spaces is that they are deliberately planned as community space, not public space, as architect Mike Brill has observed (Brill 2002). The emphasis in both design and management is on creating usable spaces that foster a strong sense of community ownership as compared to public spaces of formal parks, gridded streets, and front porches.

Traffic-protected open areas form safe play spaces for children. Residents have built play areas for their children in some of these open spaces and modified them as the kids grew older. They have also experienced some problems with nonresidents using the open spaces and picking fruit.

TABLE 2

TYPOLOGY OF OPEN SPACES FOUND IN VILLAGE HOMES

- Streets
- Central green
- Vineyards
- Orchards
- Common areas
- Playgrounds
- Drainage swales
- Community gardens
- Private courtyards
- Bicycle and pedestrian paths

Vegetation and Edible Landscape

Much of the plant material in Village Homes is either edible or native. Village Homes residents can pick fruit right outside their houses in most common areas. The edible landscape includes oranges, almonds, apricots, pears, grapes, persimmons, peaches, cherries, and plums. Community gardens located on the west side of the neighborhood provide organic produce, some of which is sold to local restaurants and markets. Annual harvest festivals bring residents together. This edible landscape has created a diverse and somewhat overgrown character to the neighborhood. Some nonresidents have commented that the overall landscape is "an eyesore" and needs a great amount of maintenance. On the other hand, residents get pleasure in seeing the seasonal cycles of nature expressed in the Village's vegetation and open spaces.

Circulation

Pedestrian and bicycle paths were laid out before and receive higher emphasis than the streets. This makes it easier to walk or bike from one part of the community to another than to drive. The greatest travel time within the neighborhood is five minutes, typically without ever crossing a road. The day care center (located in the Community Center), the Plumshire Inn restaurant, and a dance studio are no more than a five-minute walk from any house. No other services are provided in the community. Grocery stores and other services are a short bicycle ride away, although most residents use cars to shop in neighborhood centers or in downtown Davis. Large purchases generally take place in Woodland, 10 miles to the north, or in Sacramento, 15 miles east of Davis.

Open Channel Drainage[8]

The drainage system creates a network of small, creek-like channels that both hold rainwater and allow runoff to percolate back into the water table, the City of Davis' source of drinking water. During the dry summers the channels become planted play areas. The system accomplishes multiple goals. It creates a low-technology drainage system, saves infrastructure costs, and creates pleasant natural areas with visual and play value (Booth and Leavitt 1999; Girling and Helphand 1994). As a result, conventional storm sewers were not required, saving nearly $200,000 (1980 dollars) (Corbett and Corbett 2000). The ecological approach of open channel drainage (instead of catch basins and underground pipes) reportedly saved enough money to pay for most landscape improvements in the development, including walkways, gardens, and other landscape amenities.

Open channel drainage not only recharges the water table and reduces infrastructure costs for utilities but also creates a diverse landscape well suited for naturalistic play (Hart 1978; Moore 1993). These principles have been adopted and have begun to be widely implemented (see, for example, Ferguson 1998; Richman & Associates 1997). The design of a number of residential and commercial projects in Davis, including the Aspen and Willowcreek developments, incorporate open channel drainage.

8 / See the Natural Resources Defense Council website under "Selected websites" for a useful case study of the open drainage aspects of the development.

Energy Use and Conservation

A well-publicized aspect of Village Homes is its reported lower use of energy. Lenz found one-third less household energy use than in other parts of Davis (1990). This is a result of a combination of the passive solar house designs, south-facing site orientation, and south and west side shading. A dissertation at UC Davis in 1978, found that Village Homes residents consume 50 percent less energy than other residents in Davis (Hamrin 1978).

Natural heating and cooling are accomplished through both passive and active systems. While residents were not required to have solar water-heating systems, the design review committee strongly encouraged them, and Mike Corbett put them on all the homes he built. Almost every resident complied.

All houses are oriented toward the south, accommodating the use of solar panels. The design also allows south-facing windows to be shaded in the summer by overhangs and deciduous vegetation. Houses incorporate passive heating and cooling, are well insulated, and incorporate thermal mass. Solar hot water systems, when used, typically meet up to 100 percent of a home's hot water needs in the summer and above 50 percent in the winter. Street trees shade roads and reduce ambient air temperatures by as much as 10 degrees, a significant amount on hot summer days.

Water Conservation

The neighborhood is designed to conserve water through use of drought-tolerant plants and reduced use of turf areas. It employs a "hydrozoning" concept, where irrigation is applied most heavily to areas of human use (Thayer and Richman 1984). For example, larger commons have lawn for soccer practice, games, and informal gatherings, while areas along paths use native or edible vegetation. This has proved to be quite effective (Corbett and Corbett 2000).

Management

Daily management is performed by an office manager hired by the Village Homeowners Association. All residents are members of the Association (VHA). The VHA board and its various committees (which include both a design review board and an agricultural board) is a strong body that ensures local control and participation. The board of directors is involved in everything from resolving disputes among neighbors to controlling use of pesticides, to reviewing additions and remodeling of existing structures. Committees and regulations are numerous. For example, three pages of guidelines govern the community gardens, and garden coordinators are appointed to oversee different areas.

When residents move in, they receive the "Welcome to Village Homes" brochure (Village Homeowners Association 1995). More than a welcome wagon, this document lays out the history and philosophy of the neighborhood and its unique features and rules. It provides instructions for payment of homeowners' dues, noting that a reduction in fees is available for residents who maintain their portion of the common area. The board of directors makes semiannual "weed walks" to ensure that residents do their jobs. The nonprofit board also is the sole stockholder of Plumshire, Inc., a for-profit corporation set up to plan and manage nonagricultural profit-making ventures of the Association. This includes the Plumshire buildings with offices, some apartments, and a small restaurant, the Plumshire Inn.

OPPOSITE The open channel drainage system returns storm water to the water table, the source of drinking water in Davis.

Village Homes is managed by a homeowners association that meets regularly.

OPPOSITE The UC Davis agricultural fields south of Village Homes.

Community Economics

The early vision was to develop, as much as possible, an economically self-sufficient community. Moneymaking ventures were envisioned through different types of agriculture, office developments, and an inn. Only some of this has been realized. Office space owned by the Village Homeowners Association is rented, as is the Community Center. The Community Center is very popular for weddings and family reunions and is often booked. Board-sponsored events as well as free classes, parties, and meetings are exempt from fees.

Most residents are employed by the University of California or in Sacramento, the state capital. There are a few employment opportunities in the village. Those that exist are in the Plumshire office complex, at the restaurant, in the day care center, or with the Village Homeowners Association. Some residents have used the community gardens to grow and sell produce.

Food Production

Residents are the primary beneficiaries of the neighborhood's edible landscape. Lenz found that residents produce about 25 percent of their household fruit and vegetable consumption (1990). Some residents also produce their own nuts, honey, poultry, and grain. The community gardens are productive and add to the farm-like character of the neighborhood. Almond orchards are harvested in the early autumn. The community is invited to participate in this work party, and if they do, they have the opportunity to buy the almonds at a 50 percent discount. Remaining almonds are sold to other residents, and any excess is sold to commercial almond processors.

Streets are narrow and heavily planted with off-street parking spaces for visitors.

Community Organizations and Special Events

A number of special events and special interest groups are active in Village Homes. These include a "Performance Circle" of acoustical musicians, a "Secret Garden Tour," Yoga and Tai Chi classes, an Easter Egg Hunt, and a regular Potluck Brunch. Noteworthy is the annual Overhill-Westernesse Back-to-School Party. Residents of the Overhill-Westernesse common areas built a neighborhood play area in their commons and hold a back-to-school party to share it with the rest of the community.

Safety and Traffic Calming

The use of narrow and cul-de-sac streets in Village Homes appear to result in traffic-calming benefits. The need for slow streets to encourage child play and residential satisfaction has been well documented (Southworth and Ben-Joseph 1997). The long and narrow streets in Village Homes accomplish this but lead to other problems, such as lack of visitor parking.

THE DEVELOPMENT PROGRAM AND DESIGNER'S ROLE

Program Elements

Village Homes contains many unique and innovative program elements. Some of the most important include:

- 60 acres with 25 percent of site in public and community open space

- Density of 4 dwelling units/acre (approximately 7 without common landscape) compared with a density of 3–5 dwelling units/acre for developments in the vicinity

- 244 housing units (222 single-family units, 22 apartments)

- Approximately 800 residents

- Commercial office space: 4,000 square feet with 15 small businesses, including consulting and professional firms

- Small restaurant

- Dance studio

- Day care center

- Agricultural uses: including vineyard and orchards

- Greenbelts and open space: 12 acres

- Common agricultural land: 12 acres

- Two village greens, one large and one small

- Swimming pool and community center building

- Lot size: approximately 4,000 square feet

OPPOSITE Private gardens demonstrate a range of personal styles.

THE DESIGNERS

Village Homes was designed and developed by husband and wife Michael and Judy Corbett based on earlier principles of planned greenbelt communities such as Reston, Virginia, and Greenbelt, Maryland. While neither are licensed landscape architects or architects, both brought a blend of environmental training and strong social and ecological values to the project. Mike had studied architecture and Judy had done graduate studies in ecology at UC Davis, working with the famous environmental psychologist Robert Sommer. Neither had development experience, but both had a strong vision and were committed to it.

Village Homes is the result of this strong vision on the part of the designers. Its success is also due to the designers' ability to implement the vision over time. In many ways, the project has been a long-term labor of love for the Corbetts, who have fought for their vision against great odds for more than two decades. They have also lived in the community since its inception, devoted countless hours to managing and publicizing the community, and invested in local businesses within the community. Mike Corbett built and operates Plumshire Inn, a small and excellent restaurant opened in Village Homes in 1999.

To his credit, much of the site planning and landscape architecture was done by Mike Corbett. While not technically a landscape architect, he acted with the sensitivity and sensibility needed to create a well-designed landscape. The development has also benefited from the input of several licensed landscape architects and architects over the course of its development. Especially noteworthy is Rob Thayer, one of the first residents, who has, over the years, contributed his expertise as a licensed landscape architect to the design of common areas and specific landscapes. Many of his seminal ideas of sustainable design grew out of his observations while living in Village Homes (Thayer 1994, 2003). Also involved in different aspects of the design of the community over the years were architects James Zanetto (who designed and built an earth sheltered house in Village Homes in the early 1980s, and still has his architectural practice there) and Chuck McGinn; and small builders and later developers Virginia Thigpin and Bob Schneider.

Residential design is integrated with the natural and man-made landscape.

AN INFLUENTIAL
COMMUNITY DESIGN

The literature on Village Homes is almost unanimous in praise. Everything published has found the development to be highly successful. Yet much of this literature is anecdotal or based on qualitative assessments. The few more quantitative studies of Village Homes tend to support the community's successes. Given its stated goals, the place does work, yet no longitudinal long-term research has been done on the project. This limits understanding of the project's long-term benefits. It would be useful to repeat Lenz's survey or a similar study every three to five years.

THE DESIGN

The most systematic and comprehensive evaluation of Village Homes was done as a post-occupancy evaluation (POE) by Thomas Lenz (Lenz 1990).[9] According to Lenz, his research goals were to find out how Village Homes "functioned as a neighborhood, whether the design goals as stated by the developers were met, and whether residents were satisfied with their neighborhood" (Lenz 1990: 1). The data were collected between October 1988 and March 1989, and involved comparison of Village Homes to a control neighborhood in Davis.[10] Lenz also compared factors such as recycling behavior, car and bicycle trips, and household energy use between the two neighborhoods.

OPPOSITE Common areas are designed to promote creative play by children.

9 / A post-occupancy evaluation (POE) is an in-depth study of a project or place after it has been design and constructed. It typically involves a variety of methods such as observation, interviews and mapping. It often includes recommendations for design changes to improve the success of a project. See the Environmental Design Research Association (home.telepath.com/~edra) for examples of POE studies and methods.

10 / The control neighborhood was a more conventional suburban neighborhood built about the same time as Village Homes. Houses were about 20 percent larger and lots 60 percent larger than Village Homes and lacked communal open space. Lenz's study involved 89 questionnaires returned from Village Homes residents (a 37 percent return rate) and 15 from the control neighborhood residents (28 percent return).

In general Lenz found that "residents of Village Homes are more satisfied with their houses and much more satisfied with their neighborhood than their counterparts in the conventional neighborhood" (Lenz 1990: 1). Major complaints from Village Homes residents had to do with problems with solar equipment, quality of building materials, and lack of lighting in the common areas. Other concerns included the lack of parking, garages, and storage. Most appreciated was the unique social life of the neighborhood, including its communal open spaces, appropriateness for children, and opportunity for social contacts. Lenz found that residents of Village Homes socialized more and knew their neighbors better than residents in the traditional neighborhood (See Table 3).

Lenz's study raises the question of whether increased social contacts are a result of the physical design of the community or the unique kinds of people who choose to live there. Lenz found that Village Homes was comprised of a greater number of young families and what he called "special interest groups," such as students and senior citizens. He also found that the people who rated their social lives the highest tended to be Food Co-op members and community gardeners, while people who were not part of these groups socialized, recycled, and gardened less and rated the neighborhood lower on most dimensions. Lenz concludes that it is a combination of the unique values of the residents and the provision of places that bring people together that make the community more social.[11]

11 / A useful study would be to address the effect of environmental values on attachment to place. Are these values shaped by the place or do values create the sense of place? The author hypothesizes, especially in the case of Village Homes, that it is the interaction of these two that form neighborhood attitudes and a sense of belonging.

A green space along a major bike path is adjacent to a private lawn.

TABLE 3

COMPARISON OF VILLAGE HOMES AND CONVENTIONAL NEIGHBORHOOD

	VILLAGE HOMES	CONTROL NEIGHBORHOOD
DEMOGRAPHICS		
Number of households	244	54
Cars per household	1.8	2.1
Bikes per household	3.5	3.6
Family households	71.9 percent	93.3 percent
Mean household income	$51,600	$65,300
Mean house square footage	1500	1820
Percent Homeowners	86.5 percent	93.3 percent
EVALUATION OF HOUSES (0 = completely dissatisfied; 10 = completely satisfied)		
Average of all evaluated items	7.3	6.8
Overall design evaluation by respondents	7.9	7.0
EVALUATION OF NEIGHBORHOODS		
Average of all evaluated items	8.2	7.7
Overall design evaluation by respondents	8.6	7.1
EVALUATION OF FRIENDS AND SOCIALIZING		
Number of best friends within neighborhood	4	0.4
Number of friends	16	8
Number of persons known	42	17
Time spent with friends from within neighborhood (hours/week)	3.5	0.9
Time spent with friends from outside the neighborhood (hours/week)	8.7	3.7
AGRICULTURE		
Average number of fruit and vegetables grown	10	8
Average contribution to total annual consumption	24 percent	18 percent
TRANSPORTATION		
Average annual miles per car	11,300	13,400
Average miles per household	210	270
Average gas mileage of vehicles	27 mpg	23.5 mpg
Gasoline consumption per car per year	422 gallons	577 gallons
Gasoline consumption per household per year	753 gallons	1171 gallons
ENERGY CONSUMPTION		
Total yearly energy consumption per household in kilowatt hours (KWH)	44,900 KWH	67,700 KWH
RECYCLING (0) = do not recycle; 10 = always recycle)		
Glass	7.5	6.4
Paper	4.3	1.7
Organic Waste	3.4	2.0

Source: Lenz 1990.

UC Davis landscape architecture professor Patsy Owens had her students conduct a follow-up post occupancy evaluation (POE) a few years later (Owens et al. 1993).[12] Her students found similar high levels of satisfaction among residents. The three highest ranked design elements were the common areas, the bicycle and pedestrian paths, and the attractiveness of the community (Owens et al. 1993: 29). Close behind were auto circulation, closeness of houses, privacy, solar design, and open channel drainage (all above 80 percent satisfaction) (Owens et al. 1993: 29). Lowest ranked was the satisfaction with parking, which may be due to the rise in teenagers bringing a third car into the household. When asked how much longer residents planned to live in Village Homes, half answered "forever." This mirrors the strong sense of attachment to place felt by residents.

Even studies by the City of Davis now confirm its success. "The overall impression of the neighborhood is how the homes and streets recede into the lush landscape and greenbelts: a non-manicured landscape consisting of many edible plants and dominated by common areas," explained then Community Development Director Jeff Loux and Associate Planner Robert Wolcott (Loux and Wolcott 1994).

12 / Unlike Lenz, Owens had her students utilize a multimethod approach to the POE involving interviews along with observations, archival research, and recording of behavior traces. While the sample size was smaller (25 total interviews, compared to Lenz's 89), Owens' report offers a more holistic and comprehensive view of the neighborhood.

COMMUNITY

What is unique about Village Homes is how it works as a social place. The physical form of the neighborhood facilitates a cohesive and dynamic community life. For example, Lenz found in his 1990 post occupancy evaluation of Village Homes that people living in Village Homes had twice as many friends and three times as many social contacts as people living in other parts of Davis.

Another good indicator of a community is how it works for children. In the author's interviews with Judy Corbett, she emphasized this as one of the most successful aspects of the community. "It is a great place to raise kids. It offers children a sense of freedom and security. This is one of the community's greatest successes" (2000 personal communication).

In the early 1980s, the author conducted a series of observations and interviews to assess children's use of open space in Village Homes (Francis 1985, 1988). The author found in general that it provided an accessible and rich landscape that offered kids numerous opportunities for naturalistic play. One of the findings was somewhat surprising and counter to one of the core principles of Village Homes. The street was as heavily used and valued a part of the childhood landscape as the common areas. What is unique about Village Homes from a child's perspective is the diversity of places provided, from streets to play areas to natural areas, and the almost seamless access provided to these places.

The importance of Village Homes for children is exemplified by Christopher Corbett, the son of the developers, who grew up there:[13]

> Growing up in Village Homes gave me a sense of freedom and safety that would be difficult to find in the usual urban neighborhood. The orchards, swimming pool, parks, gardens, and greenbelts within Village Homes offered many stimulating, exciting, joyful places for me to play with my friends. Now that I am no longer living in Village Homes, I feel locked in by the fence in my backyard and the street in front of my house. I feel a loss of the freedom I had as a child (Corbett and Corbett 2000: 21).

This feeling was reinforced by a nonresident who works at the day care center in the Village Homes Community Center. She observes that children sometimes wander home from the day care because they are "so familiar with the environment" (Owens et al. 1993: 26).

The planners designed the public and private landscape to encourage participation by children and adults.

13 / It is interesting that Chris Corbett went on to study both landscape architecture and architecture. He has also worked with his dad on the design of the Plumshire Inn complex and plans for other new developments modeled after Village Homes.

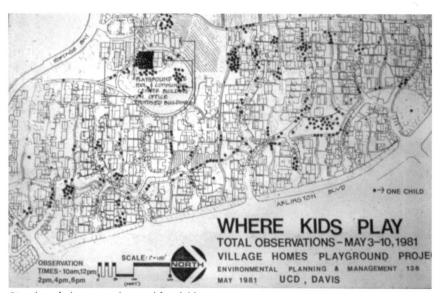

Site plan of play areas designed for children.

Children take active responsibility in helping out in community gardens.

MAINTENANCE AND MANAGEMENT

A key feature of Village Homes is the unique management system that involves residents in decision-making. Much of this system gives residents direct control over the daily management of the community. The Corbetts believed that a participatory management organization was needed for the community to be successful (2000). They chose a homeowners association model as it provided the greatest degree of local control and participation. Over the years they may have regretted this to some degree as the VHA board has gone against some of their proposals. For example, it took several years of discussion before the board agreed to develop the small restaurant complex completed in 1999. Yet the Corbetts continue to include participation as one of their essential ingredients in making sustainable communities (Corbett and Corbett 2000).

PRAISE AND COMMENTARY

Village Homes has been widely discussed and reviewed in both the professional and more popular press. Publications as diverse as *Landscape Architecture*, the *Christian Science Monitor*, *Time,* and *Newsweek* have featured the community in articles on sustainable development. Village Homes is well known abroad due to numerous documentaries aired on European and Asian television. It has also received several national design awards.

Another form of peer review is published reports by its residents on the experience of living in Village Homes. Some of the case studies published on Village Homes illustrate its unique social life. For example, Paul Tarzi, a resident of Village Homes since 1979, comments that "the open spaces and play areas are well used and provide casual meeting opportunities. You're just more accessible to your neighbors." His neighborhood group has had weekly potlucks for years. "It's something that people look forward to," he says. "Everyone has an orange flag they put out that day if they intend to come." Tarzi goes on to state, "A community is more than a physical location. It's a feeling of kinship. Living at Village Homes has enhanced our lives in many ways. I guess I could say I'm looking forward to growing old here" (Browning and Hamilton 1993: 33).

In summer 2000, a 25th-anniversary party was held for Village Homes; it was attended by 350 people, including some "alumni" who had moved away and come back to celebrate. There were speeches, music, and a slide show of the early days of the Village. For the first time, the community honored the Corbetts for their vision in founding Village Homes with a bronze plaque to be mounted on a large rock near the community center. Village Homes residents toasted the Corbetts.

Vineyard.

Orchard.

WHY DOES VILLAGE HOMES WORK?

Factors commonly cited in the literature can be briefly summarized as:[14]

• People like living there.

• It is perceived as safe.

• It is seen as a good place to raise kids.

• It is well known nationally and internationally.

• Houses have a higher resale value that makes them a good investment.

• The designers and developers live there.

• It exists in a town that is socially and environmentally aware.

• It provides a needed alternative to suburban living.

• It has meaning for residents who have a strong attachment to place.

• It encourages and fosters the participation of its residents.

• Community open spaces such as common areas, orchards, and edible gardens are highly valued by residents.

• The open channel drainage system communicates a sense of environmental stewardship and creates a unified ecological aesthetic (Mozingo 1997).

• The physical planning and design of the community works together to facilitate a sense of community.

14 / Not all of these factors were true in the beginning but have since become important.

CONSTRUCTIVE CRITICISM, PRACTICAL PROBLEMS

Most of the considerable publicity surrounding Village Homes has pointed to its successes as a development and praised its importance for other communities. Little of what has been written has been sharply critical. Yet it raises some fundamental issues surrounding the creation of community through physical design.

The National Association of Home Builders (NAHB) provides the following critique of the unrealized aspects of the Village Homes plan:

> Not all of the original design premises and expectations of Village Homes have been realized. The Davis Department of Health rejected a plan to recycle gray water for irrigating orchards. A cooperative store idea fell by the wayside, as did a central cooperative elementary school. And when federal tax credits for alternative power sources were terminated by the Reagan Administration in the 1980s, continued solar development on the Village Homes model experienced a major setback (2000).

In addition, the following have been offered as criticisms of Village Homes and its approach to community design:[15]

Shared Values or Design Determinism

Is the success of Village Homes due to its unique community design or the kind of people who have chosen to live there? This question has been raised by several observers of Village Homes. For example, landscape architect Ellen Jourset-Epstein asks in a letter to the editor to *Landscape Architecture* (2000: 11), "Is Village Homes a sharing community because of its indisputably great features? Or because

OPPOSITE Common areas are planted with colorful and diverse vegetation.

---

15 / Some of these observations are based on papers written by the author's students at UC Davis, including Landscape Architecture 220—Public Space and Public Life, Winter 2000.

The main north–south bike path is lined with fruit trees harvested by residents.

it has attracted and concentrated a population with certain shared values?" Clearly some residents decide to live there due to its physical and symbolic reflections of their environmental and social values. In the early days many residents chose to settle there due to its unique ideology and the pioneering spirit of living in a new experimental solar community. Since then, there has been a large turnover of residents and today only about 25 percent of the early residents remain, a figure that is still much higher than it is for most communities. Many people now choose to live there due to its strong property values and high quality of living. This reportedly creates some conflict between old and new residents, which sometimes needs to be mediated by the Village Homeowners Association.

Conflict with New Urbanist Principles

Clare Cooper Marcus provides a critical review of Village Homes' transformation from an early "hippie" community to now one of the most "desirable" places to live in Davis (Cooper Marcus 2000, 2001). Comparing Village Homes to New Urbanist planning, she states, "The design of this highly successful community breaks many of the rules popularized by the proponents of New Urbanism. First of all, it eschews the grid and provides access to houses via long, narrow cul-de-sacs—those 'lollipops' of 1950s suburbia much hated by proponents of New Urbanism. The green-shaded, narrow, dead-end streets save money on infrastructure, use less land, reduce urban runoff, keep the neighborhood cooler in summer, and create a quiet and safe public area where neighbors meet and children play" (Cooper Marcus 2000: 128).

Hierarchy of Open Space

Clare Cooper Marcus goes on to critique the open space design of Village Homes and compare it to the more formal, street-oriented layouts proposed by New Urbanists. She finds, based on observations, that the shared pedestrian commons or green spaces provided between houses work well for children's play, natural areas, and communal events. "This attractive environment—though accessible to outsiders riding or walking through—is definitely not a public park." She suggests that these common areas provide "a green heart" to the neighborhood. Cooper Marcus goes on to suggest that "between the designations of 'private yard' and 'public park' lies a critical category of outdoor space that might be called communal or shared" (Cooper Marcus 2000: 128).

Community garden.

What would you do differently?

Some of the criticism of Village Homes comes directly from the developers. Mike Corbett suggests that the development could be three times denser while providing the same amount of green space. Judy Corbett suggests that the community may be too big with some 800 residents. She states, "We would have had a much stronger sense of community if there were about 500 of us" (Owens et al. 1993: 20). The Corbetts disagree among themselves regarding the size of the central green area near the Community Center. Judy Corbett says, "I tend to think it would be better smaller, though Mike thinks it should stay that size. It's good for soccer practices and more spread-out activities, and it is used on weekends. It's just too big for the kind of intimacy that other open spaces seem to have fostered" (Owens et al. 1993: 20).

Where is the front door?

The site plan, which emphasizes the backyard common areas over the street, led to a dilemma in deciding where to put the front door. With the house turned away from the street, the front door was deliberately not placed on the street side. The front door could have faced the common area, since it was the major focus. The Corbetts were ambivalent about this and ultimately settled on putting the door on the side of the house. They admit that the front door "is often impossible to find" (2000: personal interview).

Lack of Open Space Use

During his informal observations over a period of several years, and more systematic observations done for this case study, the author was struck by the absence of people around Village Homes during the day. While use picked up in the evenings and on weekends, weekdays tended to find few people using the common landscape. This is also true in Aggie Village, a recently built New Urbanist community in Davis. Aggie Village has all the New Urbanist ingredients—front porches, slow traffic, pedestrian- and bicycle-oriented streets, communal open space—yet where are the people? This has been observed in many other built examples of New Urbanism. While the residents use the open spaces and paths of Village Homes more than in most new communities, some of

An ongoing management issue—to whom does the abundant fruit belong?

these spaces are seldom used. The low use may be partially due to the harsh summers in Davis, where it is not comfortable to be outdoors, especially during the day. An added factor may be the busy lives of its residents, whose time is as highly structured and over-programmed as that of their suburban counterparts in other developments. This is also true of Village Homes' children whose lives are filled up with school, sports, music lessons, computers, and TV.[16]

Whose Fruit? The Blurring of Public and Private Realms

One limitation with the design of Village Homes is the blurred boundary between public and private space. While this is responsible for much of its distinct character, with no fences between private yards and more public common areas, it has created some problems. For example, it is unclear to whom the bountiful fruit in the common areas belongs. Is it the private residents? The collection of houses around it? The entire community? The public? Visitors and even some residents are often confused by this. Common fruit trees are especially hard to identify, since they are generally near household common areas.

While the landscape is ambiguous about this, the Village Homeowners Association rules are not. They specify that "only residents of Village Homes are allowed to pick produce from the common areas. You're encouraged to introduce yourself and ask anyone you see picking if she or he is a resident. and you should politely explain to nonresidents that Village Homes is private property." Even residents are discouraged from picking fruit in other people's common areas: "Please do not pick fruit from household commons unless you see a sign inviting you to pick, and always honor signs requesting you not to pick" (Village Homeowners Association 1995: 13).

Judy Corbett commented about nonresidents harvesting their fruit, "That's a problem, but they are hard to control. We finally found a solution last year, which was simply to put up a sign saying, 'This is not your tree, please do not harvest it.' It had been picked bare the past three years but not this year" (Owens et al. 1993: 19).

16 / Designing good neighborhoods or accessible open spaces is not enough to ensure use. Socially and environmentally concerned designers also need to educate people about using these spaces and freeing up more time to use them. While Americans still have a long way to go before they are like Europeans in this regard, they are starting to use and feel more comfortable in communal space. Evidence of this can be seen in the rise of Starbucks and Borders, where hanging out is actually encouraged. This topic is the focus of another case study in this series, *Urban Open Space: Designing for User Needs*, on the theory and design of urban places.

Much of the urban forest in Village Homes is edible.

Agricultural Management

One challenge is managing intensive agriculture within a developed neighborhood. Mark Rubold, a local resident and long-term supervisor of landscape maintenance in Village Homes, comments, "the proximity of the agricultural areas to the homes poses a problem when the trees need to be sprayed. Fruit trees and grapevines need to be sprayed to control pests and disease. Often this spray drifts into public areas and the patio areas of homes" (Owens et al. 1993: 21).

Vegetation and Pest Management

With such plentiful and diverse vegetation comes a diversity of insects. In Village Homes this includes spiders (including black widows), slugs, and ants. Residents report having these in large quantities and some attribute it to the profusion of vegetation and the lack of chemical pest control. Some have called for more integrated pest management (IPM) education among gardeners and residents. As one Village Homes resident sums it up: "I'm all for integrating nature into my home, but this is ridiculous!"

Security

Village Homes has proved to be a safe neighborhood comparable to other neighborhoods in Davis. Yet it is not without its critics. A Davis police officer with the Crime Prevention Unit commented in a 1993 interview:

> If Village Homes were to be built today, it would not meet the current Davis Security Code, so many changes would need to be made. In general, the streets are too narrow for emergency vehicles to turn around, house numbers are not easily visible from the street, and lighting is poor throughout the site. Because the shrubbery is not kept pruned back from walls, there are too many places for prowlers to hide (Owens et al. 1993: 23).

These are several of the same criticisms that almost prevented Village Homes from being built. In spite of this criticism, it is one of the safer areas in Davis. Police Department records have shown that Village Homes crime rates are ninety percent below the rest of Davis (Corbett and Corbett 1983: 9).

Community garden area.

A Symbolic Community

The farm-like landscape serves as a powerful symbol for the community. Without the vineyards, orchards, and community gardens, it would appear much more like a conventional development. It demonstrates that there is a value to zoning agricultural uses within existing cities, rather than the current thinking that farms must exist apart from where people live.

Aesthetics

Village Homes has its own unique look that has been characterized as "ecological aesthetics" (Thayer 1994: 45). The landscape clearly reflects the ecological practices that guide its creation and management. While some value the "rural feeling" of the development, not all appreciate its often wild and unkempt character. The developers concede that the aesthetic of Village Homes "is not for everyone" (Corbett and Corbett 2000: personal communication). The regular "weed patrols"of the Homeowners board is evidence of the continuing struggle to find a healthy balance between wildness and order.[17]

Environmental Impacts

Much of the planning and site design was intended to be sustainable—to reduce energy use, conserve water, reduce automobile use, and create food systems. Clearly this has occurred with Village Homes. Most New Urbanist planning has similar environmental goals. Yet it is questionable if these types of development yield the same environmental benefits as Village Homes.

In a recent study at the University of Oregon funded by the National Urban and Community Forestry advisory council, researchers compared the effects of three types of neighborhood development on air, water, and urban forest quality (Girling

---

17 / An influential developer visiting Village Homes noted that "it looked like a slum" in reaction to the somewhat unkempt landscape. Most developed communities adopt a manicured approach to their landscape and reinforce this through strict regulations requiring a high level of maintenance. Village Homes took a different approach where natural aesthetic is more highly valued. But it does raise the issue of the aesthetics of ecological design. Rob Thayer (1994) has provided a useful theory that suggests that making sustainability visible is valued by the public. Clearly, the high satisfaction of Village Homes by its residents proves this true.

et al. 2000). They did extensive modeling of a traditional suburban development, a typical gridded New Urbanist development, and an open-space-oriented development modeled largely after Village Homes. They found that the traditional and New Urbanist developments had very similar environmental impacts in the amounts of impervious surface, runoff, and energy use; however, only the Village Homes-type development produced significant improvements in air, water, and forest quality. This study points out the need for more comparative studies that look across cases.

Replication

The most common and troubling criticism of the project is that it has not been replicated, at least in the United States. Residential developments oriented around open spaces, such as Village Homes, are more commonly found in Europe, including Scandinavia and Britain. Even the developers acknowledge that "there is nothing like it anywhere" (Corbett and Corbett 2000: personal communication). Village Homes has even spawned developers among its residents who have chosen not to replicate its successes. When asked why, the response is that "it would be too risky." John Whitcombe, one of Davis' leading residential developers, is not surprised no one has built a project as revolutionary as Village Homes. He suggests that "the main reason there aren't more Village Homes is there's only one Mike Corbett" (Fitch 1999: 12). Chuck Roe, another local developer, has suggested that Village Homes has not been replicated due to the requirements now for higher density development in Davis and the ongoing concerns of City Public Works engineers regarding drainage and layout (Roe 2003: personal communication).

City of Davis planner Doris Michael suggests that it is due to the fact that "it is too expensive" (Owens et al. 1993: 17). She attributes the lack of replication to "not all people feeling comfortable living so close to others." Expense and density are common fears of developers. Yet the reality of development has proved that these are more myth than fact.

Planners Loux and Wolcott have observed: "Many citizens throughout the city look with pride to Village Homes and question why no similar model has been built in the past 20 years" (1994: 6). The two planners suggest that the reasons for this are increases in land prices and changes in home styles and tastes. City standards in Davis and elsewhere remain a substantial barrier for a developer wanting to build a similar project.

Mike Corbett offers an assessment of why the project has not been reproduced. "The problem is not that the public does not want it. They come here and see what we have done and say, 'Why isn't everybody doing this?' But developers are so closed-minded. They continue to build thousands of places where you can't get around without a car" (Jackson 1999: 79).

Even replicating the project in Davis has been difficult. Judy Corbett points out, "the present City Council does not hesitate to brag to other countries about how wonderful their Village Homes is, but they do not seem to do much to enable anything like it to be built here again" (Owens et al. 1993: 19). Some of the ideas, such as open channel drainage and natural landscape, have been used in later developments in Davis, but no one has attempted to replicate the community in whole. For now, it is a one-of-a-kind project. Perhaps what is most important, rather than total replication, is that the successes of Village Homes be reproduced elsewhere.

A typical cul-de-sac with off-street parking. Limited storage and garage space is an ongoing problem for residents.

PRACTICAL PROBLEMS OF A PIONEER DESIGN

With its many successes and pioneering design and planning features, Village Homes has not been without its problems. Many of these are minor design flaws, yet several raise significant issues for designing similar sustainable communities.

Lack of garages

Inadequate storage space has created visual clutter. Judy Corbett has commented, "I would have no carports. Those seem to have just gotten messy, and people complain about lack of storage. Garages would work much better" (Owens et al. 1993: 20).

Lack of parking

On-street and visitor parking is sometimes limited.

Lack of privacy

While the amount of privacy provided in Village Homes was highly rated by residents (Owens et al. 1993), it may be a barrier to some moving into the community.

Low density

The developers and most observers agree that the same success could have been achieved with a higher density.

Affordability and gentrification

The developers worked hard in the early stages to develop a diverse economic and social population of about 15 percent low-income residents, through mechanisms such as allowing residents to make down payments on houses with one year of their labor. Despite such great efforts to provide affordable housing opportunities, economic and social diversity have been limited. As home values have escalated, so too has the number of professional residents. While rental apartments, the co-op house, and small houses create a sense of diversity, economic and social diversity are as limited in the community as in the larger city of Davis.

Sustaining participation

As the community has matured it has been difficult to sustain the level of involvement of the early days. This may be due to the turnover of residents and that the pioneer spirit has faded over time. For example, the Village Homeowners Association (VHA) in its newsletter (March 1999) complained about the shortage of votes to conduct Board elections.[18]

Small lots and houses

One POE of Village Homes found that most residents interviewed would prefer bigger lots or houses to accommodate more storage area (Owens et al. 1993: 31).

Legibility and interpretation

To capitalize on its draw as a destination for ecotourists, an information center could be provided to explain how the community came about and why it is unique.

Sustaining the agricultural landscape

The head gardener has commented that "crops were intended to generate income but over the years they have cost to maintain them" (Owens et al. 1993: 22). Observations confirm this, as fruit and grapes in many areas are often left to rot.

---

18 / Village Homes bylaws require that a minimum of one-quarter of VHA homeowners cast ballots in the annual elections. In 1999, only 19 out of the required 56 cast ballots in the annual election of the Board of Directors. In addition to calls in the newsletter to vote, the VHA office manager "pedaled around the Village with a fistful of ballots looking for and finding a gaggle of 20 residents who had not yet voted" (VHA Newsletter, March 1999). Like any community, participation varies by year and depending on issues, but clearly there is not as much involvement as in the early days of the neighborhood. Judy Corbett observes, "when things are going well in the community, people become uninterested in participating."

A community orchard to the left, and community garden to right.

VILLAGE HOMES:
CONCLUSIONS AND RECOMMENDATIONS

Most, if not all, of the design and planning principles discussed earlier are directly applicable to other projects. Most noteworthy are:

- Participation
- Open channel drainage
- Emphasis on open space
- Diversity of open space types
- Communal space
- Child-oriented landscapes
- Hydrozoning
- Mixed use village/community center
- Emphasis on pedestrians and bikes first, cars second

There are some comparable developments to Village Homes worth noting. Perhaps the closest philosophically is The Woodlands in Texas, also designed in the early 1970s (Wallace McHarg Roberts and Todd 1974). Most physically similar to Village Homes is the more recent Prairie Crossing, a 667-acre development in Grayslake, Illinois, north of Chicago (Corbett and Corbett 2000). Prairie Crossing puts similar emphasis on agriculture and open space, with 150 acres set aside for farmland among its 317 home sites. It also uses a natural drainage system. Other recent examples that share similarities to Village Homes are Coffee Creek in Indiana (being designed by architect William McDonough), Haymount in Virginia, and Civano in Arizona. One might also compare Village Homes to two other well-known planned communities—The Sea Ranch, also in California, and Seaside in Florida.[19]

OPPOSITE The Plumshire Inn at Village Homes is a popular restaurant.

19 / See *A Case Study Method for Landscape Architecture* (Francis 1999a, 2000), which presents The Sea Ranch as a case study.

Common areas and pathways intersect.

ISSUES, PLANS, AND CHALLENGES

If Village Homes was being designed today, some thirty years later, how should it be different? Given its great success, one could argue that it should be designed exactly the same. There are so many things that work well about this place; why change them? Yet there have been many advances in the basic design principles pioneered in this project. For example, we know more about how to design natural drainage systems and make them larger, more visible parts of communities (Richman & Associates 1997).

When asked what she would do differently, Judy Corbett commented, "build the commercial area first rather than wait until the end" (2000: personal communication). She observes that NIMBYism ("not in my back yard") does set in, and residents become resistant to change and new ideas. Just like the City of Davis was a barrier to implementing the Corbetts' ideas, residents were reluctant to approve their plans for completion of the Village Center. Perhaps the biggest challenge to the community is how it can maintain the strong sense of social design as the place ages and matures. The residents will have to work especially hard if they want to sustain this over time.

THE VILLAGE HOMES INFLUENCE

The ideas and principles embodied in Village Homes can be used in many other situations. Village Homes has influenced many designers and developers, and has also inspired development of important theory and built practices of sustainable community design. An important example is Rob Thayer's work on sustainable landscape architecture, directly influenced by his 25 years of living in Village Homes (Thayer 1994).

Writing in his award-winning article in 1977, which introduced Village Homes to design professionals, landscape architect Thayer suggested that it may not be appropriate to make Village Homes a model for all community design. "It may be unwise to suggest that Village Homes is a generalizable case study. A large percentage of homeowners live there as an experiment." He goes on to conclude, "Village Homes will make a significant contribution to progress in community design, whether it stabilizes as a neighborhood and true product of environmental awareness or serves as a continually evolving laboratory for conservation and community in environmental design. As Buckminister Fuller might say, 'Village Homes is perhaps less a noun and more a verb'" (Thayer 1977: 122).

It is clear that the experimental period of the project is now past, and it has become more established and even institutionalized as a community. It now serves as a living example of sustainable community design and an ongoing laboratory for research and design innovation.

Village Homes has also inspired development of community design and livability principles that have become more mainstream. Perhaps the most direct translation of this is the Ahwahnee Principles developed by the Local Government Commission (LGC) in Sacramento (1991). They resulted from a gathering of leading community designers convened by Judy Corbett, executive director of LGC, in the late 1980s. Attending this meeting in the Corbetts' Village Homes living room were Peter Calthorpe, Andres Duany, and Michael Corbett, among others. Together they developed a list of the main principles that they believed should guide sustainable community design. These were refined at a subsequent meeting of mayors and local officials in the historic Ahwahnee Hotel in Yosemite Valley (see Table 4).

A common area.

Edible vegetation.

DIRECTIONS FOR FUTURE WORK

Mike Corbett summarizes the importance of his and Judy Corbett's labor of love in this way:

> We do not view Village Homes as an ideal. We see it as a practical step in the right direction. Just as the houses and the quality of life within Village Homes have been improved as we have gained experience, we hope that future developments will be improved to become largely self-sufficient neighborhoods. Most of the necessary techniques, equipment and knowledge is now available to do this. The challenge is to combine these many simple, practical and economical steps so they work together (Corbett 1983: 9).

As we search to find concrete ways to reduce sprawl and create community, Village Homes provides a guiding light. It is not that it needs to be replicated in whole, but its components when combined together can make livable and sustainable communities. Village Homes is significant because it demonstrates clearly the power of landscape, the importance of landscape architecture in providing a sustainable future, and how community can be successfully created by design.

TABLE 4

Ahwahnee Principles

Existing patterns of urban and suburban development seriously impair our quality of life. The symptoms are: more congestion and air pollution resulting from our increased dependence on automobiles; the loss of precious open space; the need for costly improvements to roads and public services; the inequitable distribution of economic resources; and the loss of a sense of community. By drawing upon the best from the past and the present, we can plan communities that will more successfully serve the needs of those who live and work within them. Such planning should adhere to certain fundamental principles.

COMMUNITY PRINCIPLES

1. All planning should be in the form of complete and integrated communities containing housing, shops, work places, schools, parks and civic facilities essential to the daily life of the residents.
2. Community size should be designed so that housing, jobs, daily needs and other activities are within easy walking distance of each other.
3. As many activities as possible should be located within easy walking distance of transit stops.
4. A community should contain a diversity of housing types to enable citizens from a wide range of economic levels and age groups to live within its boundaries.
5. Businesses within the community should provide a range of job types for the community's residents.
6. The location and character of the community should be consistent with a larger transit network.
7. The community should have a center focus that combines commercial, civic, cultural and recreational uses.
8. The community should contain an ample supply of specialized open space in the form of squares, greens and parks whose frequent use is encouraged through placement and design.
9. Public spaces should be designed to encourage the attention and presence of people at all hours of the day and night.

10. Each community or cluster of communities should have a well-defined edge, such as agricultural greenbelts or wildlife corridors, permanently protected from development.

11. Streets, pedestrian paths and bike paths should contribute to a system of fully-connected and interesting routes to all destinations. Their design should encourage pedestrian and bicycle use by being small and spatially defined by buildings, trees and lighting; and by discouraging high speed traffic.

12. Wherever possible, the natural terrain, drainage and vegetation of the community should be preserved with superior examples contained within parks or greenbelts.

13. The community design should help conserve resources and minimize waste.

14. Communities should provide for the efficient use of water through the use of natural drainage, drought tolerant landscaping and recycling.

15. The street orientation, the placement of buildings and the use of shading should contribute to the energy efficiency of the community.

REGIONAL PRINCIPLES

1. The regional land-use planning structure should be integrated within a larger transportation network built around transit rather than freeways.

2. Regions should be bounded by and provide a continuous system of greenbelt/wildlife corridors to be determined by natural conditions.

3. Regional institutions and services (government, stadiums, museums, etc.) should be located in the urban core.

4. Materials and methods of construction should be specific to the region, exhibiting a continuity of history and culture and compatibility with the climate to encourage the development of local character and community identity.

IMPLEMENTATION PRINCIPLES

1. The general plan should be updated to incorporate the above principles.

2. Rather than allowing developer-initiated, piecemeal development, local governments should take charge of the planning process. General plans should designate where new growth, infill or redevelopment will be allowed to occur.

3. Prior to any development, a specific plan should be prepared based on these planning principles.

4. Plans should be developed through an open process and participants in the process should be provided visual models of all planning proposals.

Source: Local Government Commission (LGC) 1991; www.lgc.org

BIBLIOGRAPHY

Alexander, C., S. Ishikawa, and M. Silverstein. 1977. *A Pattern Language: Towns, Buildings, Construction.* New York: Oxford University Press.

Bainbridge, D., J. Corbett, and J. Hofacre. 1979. *Village Homes Solar House Designs.* Emmaus, PA: Rodale Press.

Booth, D. B., and J. Leavitt. 1999. Field Evaluation of Permeable Pavement Systems for Improved Storm Water Management. *APA Journal* 65(3).

Brill, M. 2002. Problems with Mistaking Community Life for Public Life. *Places.* 14. 2: 48–55.

Browning, B., and K. Hamilton. 1993. Village Homes: A Model Solar Community Proves its Worth. *In Context: A Quarterly Journal of Sustainable Culture.* Spring, 33.

Calthorpe, P. 1993. *The Next American Metropolis: Ecology, Community, and the American Dream.* New York: Princeton Architectural Press.

Calthorpe, P., W. Fulton, and R. Fishman. 2000. *The Regional City: New Urbanism and the End of Sprawl.* Washington, DC: Island Press.

Cooper Marcus, C. 2000. Looking Back at Village Homes. *Landscape Architecture* 90(7):125, 128.

———. 2001. The Neighborhood Approach to Building Community: A Different Perspective on Smart Growth. *Western City Magazine.* March.

Cooper Marcus, C., and M. Barnes, eds. 1999. *Healing Gardens.* New York: Wiley.

Corbett, M. N. 1981. *A Better Place to Live.* Emmaus, PA: Rodale Press.

Corbett, M. N., and J. Corbett. 1983. *Toward Better Neighborhood Design.* Human Ecology Monograph Series. Lansing: College of Human Ecology, Michigan State University.

———. 2000. *Designing Sustainable Communities: Learning from Village Homes.* Washington, DC: Island Press.

Cowan, S., and S. Van der Ryn. 1996. *Ecological Design.* Washington, DC: Island Press.

Duany, A., E. Plater-Zyberk and J. Speck. 2000. *Suburban Nation: The Rise of Sprawl and the Decline of the American Dream.* New York: North Point Press.

Ferguson, B. K. 1998. *Introduction to Stormwater.* New York: Wiley.

Fitch, M. 1999. Growing Pains: Thirty Years in the History of Davis. Unpublished manuscript. Davis: City of Davis.

Francis, M. 1985. Children's Use of Open Space in Village Homes. *Children's Environments Quarterly* 1(4): 36–38.

———. 1988. Negotiating Between Child and Adult Design Values. *Design Studie*s 9 (2): 67–75.

———. 1995. *Open Space Oriented Development.* Davis: Center for Design Research.

———. 1999a. A Case Study Method for Landscape Architecture. Washington, DC: Landscape Architecture Foundation.

———. 1999b. Proactive Practice: Visionary Thought and Participatory Action in Environmental Design. *Places* 12 (1): 60–68.

———. 1999c. Planning in Place. *Places* 12 (2).

———. 2000. A Case Study Method for Landscape Architecture. *Landscape Journal* 19 (2).

———. 2003. *Urban Open Spaces: Designing for User Needs.* Washington DC: Island Press.

Francis, M., S. Jones, and K. Dawson. 1989. *The Davis Greenway: A Conceptual Plan for Open Space and Wildlife Habitat for the City of Davis, California.* Davis: UC Davis Center for Design Research.

Francis, M., L. Cashdan, and L. Paxson. 1984. *Community Open Spaces.* Washington, DC: Island Press.

Francis, M., and R. Hester, eds. 1990. *The Meaning of Gardens.* Cambridge: MIT Press.

Girling, C. L., and K. Helphand. 1994. *Yard, Street, Park: The Design of Suburban Open Space.* New York: Wiley.

Girling, C., R. Kellett, D. Popko, J. Rochefort, and C. Roe. 2000. *Green Neighborhoods: Planning and Design Guidelines for Air, Water and Urban Forest Quality.* Eugene, OR: Center for Housing Innovation.

Hamrin, J. 1978. Two Energy Conserving Communities: Implications for Public Policy. Ph.D. Dissertation. UC Davis.

Hart, R. 1978. *Children's Experience of Place.* New York: Irvington.

Hayden, D. 1995. *The Power of Place.* Cambridge: MIT Press.

Howard, E. 1965. *Garden Cities for Tomorrow.* Cambridge: MIT Press.

Jackson, D. 1999. Back to the Garden: A Suburban Dream. *Time.* February 22.

Jourset-Epstein, E. 2000. Letter to the Editor. *Landscape Architecture* (90) 9: 9, 11. September.

Lang, J. 1994. *Urban Design: The American Experience.* New York: Van Nostrand Reinhold.

Lenz, T. 1990. A Post-Occupancy Evaluation of Village Homes, Davis, California. Unpublished Master's Thesis. Technical University of Munich.

Local Government Commission (LGC). 1991. *The Awhahnee Principles.* Sacramento: LGC.

———. 1999. *Village Homes: A Model Project.* Sacramento: LGC.

Loux, J., and R. Wolcott. 1994. Innovation in Community Design: The Davis Experience. Unpublished Monograph. City of Davis.

Lyle, J. 1996. *Regenerative Design for Sustainable Development.* New York: Wiley.

Meltzer, G. 2000. Cohousing: Verifying the Importance of Community in the Application of Environmentalism. *Journal of Architectural and Planning Research* (17) 2: 110–132.

Moore, R. C. 1993. *Plants for Play: A Plant Selection Guide for Children's Outdoor Environments.* Berkeley, CA: MIG Communications.

Mozingo, L. A. 1997. The Aesthetics of Ecological Design: Seeing Science as Culture. *Landscape Journal* Spring. 46–59.

National Association of Home Builders (NAHB). 2000. *Smart Growth Resources: Village Homes.* Washington, DC: NAHB.

Owens, P., et. al. 1993. *A Post Occupancy Evaluation of Village Homes.* Davis: UC Davis, Center for Design Research.

Relph, T. 1986. *Place and Placelessness.* London: Pion.

Richman & Associates. 1997. Start at the Source: Residential Site Planning & Design Guidance for Stormwater Quality Protection. Bay Area Stormwater Management Agencies Association (BASMAA).

Southworth, M., and E. Ben-Joseph. 1997. *Streets and the Shaping of Towns and Cities.* New York: McGraw Hill.

Stansel, T. 1999. Conserving Community: Prairie Crossing and Tryon Farms are National Role Models of Green Housing. *Conscious Choice.* September.

Stein, C. 1989. *Toward New Towns for America.* Cambridge: MIT Press.

Stitt, F. 1999. *Ecological Design Handbook: Sustainable Strategies for Architecture, Landscape Architecture, Interior Design, and Planning.* New York: McGraw Hill.

Thompson, G. F., and F. Steiner, eds. 1997. *Ecological Design and Planning.* New York: Wiley.

Thayer, R. L. Jr., 1977. Designing an Experimental Solar Community. *Landscape Architecture* 16 (5): 223–228.

———. 1989. The Experience of Sustainable design. *Landscape Journal.* 8 (2).

———. 1994. *Gray World: Green Heart.* New York: Wiley.

———. 2003. *Lifeplace: Bioregional Thought and Practice.* Berkeley: University of California Press.

Thayer, Jr., R. L. and T. Richman, 1984. Water-Conserving Landscape Design. In *Energy Conserving Site Design*, G. McPherson, ed. Washington, DC: Landscape Architecture Foundation.

Turner, M. 2000. Village Homes Dream Lives on 25 Years Later. *Davis Enterprise.* September 11.

Ulrich, R. 1985. Human Responses to Vegetation and Landscapes. *Landscape and Urban Planning.* 13: 29–44.

Vernez-Moudon, A. *Public Streets for Public Use.* New York: Columbia University Press.

Village Homeowners Association. 1995. New Homeowners Guide.

——. 1995. Welcome to Village Homes.

——. 1999. Community Garden Guidelines.

Wackernagel, M., and W. Rees. 1996. *Our Ecological Footprint: Reducing Human Impact on the Earth.* Philadelphia: New Society Publishers.

Wallace, McHarg, Roberts and Todd, Inc. 1974. Woodlands New Community: An Ecological Plan. Woodlands, TX.

Wilson, A., J. L. Uncapher, L. A. McManigal, L. Hunter Lovins, M. Cureton, and W. D. Browning. 1998. *Green Development: Integrating Ecology and Real Estate.* New York: Wiley.

Woodbridge, S. 1995. New Ecoburbs. *On the Ground.* Winter/Spring.

PHOTO CREDITS

Cover   Tom Lamb

Frontispiece
and Title Page   Gardens in Village Homes are planted with edible and native plants, by Mark Francis

ALL PHOTOS ARE BY TOM LAMB, UNLESS OTHERWISE NOTED.

Mary Bedard   14, 43

Judy Corbett   x, 17, 18, 28 left and right, 40, 58 top

Mark Francis   xiii bottom left, 15, 19, 22, 31 bottom, 50, 57 left, 58 bottom

SOURCES OF INFORMATION

Village Homeowners Association
2661 Portage Bay, Davis, CA 95616. tel 530.753.6345

Judy Corbett, Local Government Commission
1414 K St, Suite 250, Sacramento, CA 95814. www.lgc.org

Michael Corbett, Town Planners
2659 Portage Bay East, Davis, CA 95616. tel 530.750.2939

CASE STUDIES OF VILLAGE HOMES ON THE WEB

Local Government Commission: www.lgc.org/villagehomes/index.html

MIT Department of Urban Planning: www.libraries.mit.edu/guides/subjects/architecture/architects/prf/prf-name.html

National Association of Home Builders (members only): www.nahb.net

Natural Resources Defense Council, Stormwater Strategies, Community Responses to Runoff Pollution, Natural Drainage at Village Homes: www.nrdc.org/water/pollution/storm/chap9.asp#DAV

Rocky Mountain Institute: www.rmi.org/sitepages/pid209.asp

Time Magazine, Heroes of the Planet: www.time.com/time/reports/environment/heroes/heroesgallery/0,2967,corbett,00.html

U. S. Department of Energy Center of Excellence in Sustainable Development: www.sustainable.doe.gov/success/village.shtml

The Vital Signs Curriculum Materials Project, UC Berkeley: www.arch.ced.berkeley.edu/vitalsigns/workup/siegel_house/vh_bkgd.html

SELECTED WEBSITES

American Community Gardening Association: www.communitygarden.org

American Institute of Architects: www.aia.org

American Planning Association: www.planning.org

Congress for New Urbanism: www.cnu.org

Landscape Architecture Foundation: www.LAfoundation.org

Lincoln Institute of Land Policy: www.lincolninst.edu

Trust for Public Land: www.tpl.org

University of Toronto CLIP site: www.clr.utoronto.ca/virtuallib/clip/

Urban Land Institute: www.uli.org

INDEX

ABOUT THE AUTHOR

Mark Francis, a Fellow of the American Society of Landscape Architects, is professor of landscape architecture at the University of California, Davis, and senior design consultant with Moore Iacofano Goltsman. Trained in landscape architecture and urban design at Berkeley and Harvard, he is author of more than sixty articles and book chapters translated into a dozen languages. His books include *Community Open Spaces* (Island, 1984), *The Meaning of Gardens* (MIT, 1990), *Public Space* (Cambridge, 1992), and *The California Landscape Garden: Ecology, Culture and Design* (California, 1999). He has received eight Honor and Merit awards and a Centennial Medallion from the American Society of Landscape Architects for his design, planning, research, and writing. His work has focused on the use and meaning of the built and natural landscape. Much of this research has utilized a case study approach to study parks, gardens, public spaces, streets, nearby nature, and urban public life. He is past president of the Environmental Design Research Association, is associate editor of the *Journal of Architectural & Planning Research* and serves on the editorial boards of *Landscape Journal, Journal of Planning Literature, Environment & Behavior, Children's and Youth Environments,* and *Design-Research Connections.*

AUTHOR ACKNOWLEDGMENTS

This case study follows a methodology and format developed previously for the Landscape Architecture Foundation (LAF). It is one of three prototype case studies (place-based, issue-based and teaching) developed by the author for LAF's *Land and Community Design Case Study Series*. It is intended both as a place-based case study of Village Homes and as a prototype case study that will aid others in developing cases of designed landscapes.

The preparation of this case study was funded by a JJR Research Grant and the Graham Foundation for Advanced Studies in the Fine Arts. In addition, support was provided by the University of California Agricultural Experiment Station. Tom Lamb, Lamb Studios, provided most of the Village Homes photographs in this publication as a pro bono effort for LAF. I would like to express my gratitude to the designers and developers of Village Homes, Judy and Mike Corbett, whose openness, self-criticism, and enthusiasm greatly aided preparation of this case study. I would also like to thank Rob Thayer, my colleague at UC Davis and longtime Village Homes resident, for his important research and insight over the years regarding Village Home and its significance for landscape architecture. My students at UC Davis have also been important observers of Village Homes and have greatly informed my own views of the place. Mary Bedard, Judy Corbett, Randall Fleming, and Rob Thayer provided useful comments on an earlier draft of this report.

I am grateful to the LAF and its board for commissioning this study and for their overall support of the case study initiative in landscape architecture. I would especially like to thank Frederick Steiner, former LAF president and dean at the University of Texas in Austin, and LAF executive director Susan Everett for their assistance and encouragement. I would like to express my gratitude to Heather Boyer of Island Press and Jan Cigliano of Academy Press for helping bring this story to life.

LANDSCAPE ARCHITECTURE FOUNDATION ACKNOWLEDGMENTS

Major support to LAF and its programs is provided by the American Society of Landscape Architects, ValleyCrest Landscape Development, Landscape Forms, Landscape Structures, Sasaki Associates, The Brickman Group, EDAW, Design Workshop, The HOK Planning Group, JJR, Canterbury International, LM Scofield Company, ONA, The Saratoga Associates and Robert Bristol, Civitas, Scott Byron and Company, Hunter Industries, Cold Spring Granite Company, EDSA, Sitecraft, Laurance S. Rockefeller, and the Bomanite Corporation.

Lead donors offering support to LAF programs include Burton Associates, Lannert Group, Dura Art Stone, Wyss Associates, Estrada Land Planning, NUVIS, Wallace Roberts & Todd, Carol R. Johnson Associates, Leatzow & Associates, Kim Lighting, The Toro Company Irrigation Division, SWA Group, LDR International, Glatting Jackson Kercher Anglin Lopez Rinehart, The Care of Trees, Signe Nielsen, Nimrod Long and Associates, Hughes, Good, O'Leary & Ryan, dhm design corporation, Hargreaves Associates, Meisner + Associates Land Vision, Peter Walker & Partners, Smith & Hawken, and other donors.

The Graham Foundation for Advanced Studies in the Fine Arts provided generous support at a critical juncture in the development of the case studies. We are deeply indebted to the Graham Foundation and its executive director, Richard Solomon, for their sage advice and early support.

LAF commissioned Mark Francis to develop the Case Study Method in Landscape Architecture in 1997, and subsequently to write the prototypes for each of the case study types: project-based, issue-based and teaching. In the Case Study Method in Landscape Architecture, Mark went beyond merely creating a format for future case study researchers, creating in addition an ambitious vision for the program. We are grateful to Mark for the scope of his vision, his commitment, persistence, and leadership on the cases study series.

Mark Francis developed the case study series concept with the intent of creating an online archive of case study abstracts; case study compendia organized by type; case study institutes organized by project type or geographic region; sessions at annual meetings to focus on the case study method, comparative analysis, and theory building; and eventually, as the series develops, a national archive of case study projects related to the built and natural environment; a national conference on case studies that brings together national organizations; and public policy symposia that link case study findings to public policy issues.

The Land & Community Design Case Study Series National Advisory Council helped to shape the series during its formation. Our thanks to members Kathleen A. Blaha, L. Susan Everett, Mark Francis, Richard S. Hawks, Joe A. Porter, William H. Roberts, George L. Sass, Frederick R. Steiner, and Joanne M. Westphal. Vice-president for information and research Gary A. Hack provided oversight and shaped the series as it evolved, and was instrumental in identifying and selecting a publishing partner. Frederick R. Steiner served as the vice president for information and research during the gestation of the case study series and as LAF president during a critical stage in its development. We appreciate his on-going participation and guidance. The LAF California Landscape Architectural Student Scholarship Fund, known as the CLASS Fund, AILA Yamagami Hope Fellowship, supported the publication by LAF of the Case Study Method in Landscape Architecture.

The JJR Research Fund supported the research and writing for the site-based case study prototype, Village Homes: A Community by Design. We are grateful to Tom Lamb of Lamb Studio, who generously donated his craft in providing the new photographs of Village Homes.

Finally, LAF wishes to thank the anonymous reviewers for their thoughtful comments and guidance, and the peer reviewers who provided insights and suggestions to each of the authors.

To produce the first books in the series, art director Mihae Kim and the design staff of the Gimga Group worked patiently with LAF on the graphic design as the series concept evolved, and supplied the creative design that gives the series its distinctively elegant appearance. Academy Press publisher and editor Jan Cigliano provided skilled organization and timely project management in working with the authors, publisher, graphic designer, and LAF on three publications simultaneously.

Heather Boyer, Island Press editor, graciously offered support and counsel throughout the development of the case study series and we are indebted to her for her invaluable and ongoing assistance. Island Press publisher and vice president Dan Sayre offered encouragement from the beginning and was willing to take a risk on a highly visual publication.